# Hoplites: The History and Legacy of the Ancient Greek Soldiers Who Revolutionized Infantry Warfare

## By Charles River Editors

**An illustration of a hoplite**

## About Charles River Editors

**Charles River Editors** is a boutique digital publishing company, specializing in bringing history back to life with educational and engaging books on a wide range of topics. Keep up to date with our new and free offerings with this 5 second sign up on our weekly mailing list, and visit Our Kindle Author Page to see other recently published Kindle titles.

We make these books for you and always want to know our readers' opinions, so we encourage you to leave reviews and look forward to publishing new and exciting titles each week.

# Introduction

# Hoplites

"The walls of Sparta were its young men, and its borders the points of their spears." – attributed to King Agesilaos

Although the armies of the ancient Greek, or "Hellenic", city-states (*poleis*, singular *polis*) included both cavalry (*hippeis*) and light infantry (*psiloi, peltastes, gymnetes*), their mainstay was undoubtedly the heavy infantry known today as hoplites. Armed to the teeth with their distinctive round shield (*aspis* or *hoplon*), high-crested helmet (*corys*) and long spear (*dory*), the hoplites were some of the most efficient soldiers of their time. They fought in the tight phalanx formation, and beyond the confines of their small poleis, Greek hoplites were also prized as mercenaries throughout the ancient world.

Most historians believe that the hoplite became the dominant infantry soldier in nearly all the Greek city-states around the 8th century BCE. Hoplites were responsible for acquiring their own equipment, so not every hoplite might have been equally armed, but considering the style of warfare, they needed as much uniformity as possible. Like most infantry outside of Greece, the hoplites also carried spears, but while the Persian weapons were short and light for example, the Greek spears were thick shafts anywhere between seven and nine feet long. These spears were topped by a 9-inch spearhead, with a "lizard-sticker" buttspike at the bottom which could be used as a secondary spearhead if the main weapon was snapped off, or to plant the spear upright when at rest. Each hoplite also carried a shortsword, designed specifically for thrusting in the close confines of a melee (the Spartan weapon, the *xiphos,* was so short as to be virtually a dagger, its blade barely over a foot long).

Unlike the Persian infantry, the hoplites did not carry bows. Though the Greeks did employ light infantry, in the form of slingers, javelineers and archers, their role was extremely secondary to that of the heavy infantry. This was largely due to the armor which each hoplite wore into battle, which consisted of bronze greaves covering the wearer from ankle to knee, a skirt of leather or quilted linen to protect the groin area, and a heavy breastplate made either of bronze or quilted linen under overlapping bronze scales. To protect their heads, the hoplites wore the famous helmet that is perhaps their most iconic feature, a full-face bronze helmet with high flaring cheek-pieces and a thick nasal that obscured and protected their faces completely, topped by a horsehair crest that added another foot to their height. Helmets were worn front-to-back for line infantry and sideways for officers, to make them more recognizable to their own troops in the heat of battle.

Armored from head to foot in iron and bronze, the hoplite was the tank of his age, but the most important feature of his equipment was undoubtedly his shield. Weighing in at over 30 pounds, the *hoplon* or *aspis* was a great wooden bowl over three feet in diameter, made of heavy oak fronted with bronze and covering each hoplite from knee to neck, as well as providing a significant overlap with the shields of his companions in the battle-line. There could be no standing off and engaging the enemy at a distance with the Greek hoplites carrying shortswords and thrusting spears, and because of the weight of their equipment (which was up to 70-90 pounds all told).

For the Greeks, a hoplite was only as strong as the hoplite next to him; without hoplites on the sides, both flanks were exposed, and heavy infantry units are not mobile. Thus, they implemented the phalanx formation, one of history's most important military innovations. The phalanx was a line of infantry as wide across as the battlefield dictated, anything from five to 30 men deep, with each rank of men officered by a veteran. The formation also included an additional, expert file-closer at the back of each file, to keep the formation cohesive.

The phalanx advanced slowly to maintain its tight formation and unit cohesion, speeding up in unison just before reaching combat. The vast hoplite shields overlapped one another significantly, forming an uninterrupted wall of oak and bronze over which the first rank, while holding out their shields, would use their short swords to stab at the enemy in front of him, while the ranks immediately behind the first rank would slash at enemies with their spears over the top of the first line. Because each soldier's right flank was shielded by his companion's shield (all shields were strapped to the left arm, to preserve the integrity of the formation; left-handed fighters did not exist), the phalanx, especially in the case of less well-trained units, had a tendency to edge to the right, which the Greeks countered by placing their elite troops to the right as a bulwark. The rows in back of the first line would also use their shields to help hold up the hoplites in the front and help them maintain their balance. The formation and method of attack was designed to physically overpower the enemy and scare them, lowering their morale. The phalanx as a fighting unit fell out of favor by the height of the Roman Empire, but the principles behind it remained in use for subsequent infantry formations lasting past the American Civil War. As the Greeks relied on the hoplite to defend other hoplites and concentrate their attack, infantry units in the gunpowder age relied on concentrated gunfire to stun and scare the enemy. And as military commanders learned time and again throughout the ages, if soldiers were not packed shoulder to shoulder in a tight formation, they were far more likely to flee.

Ultimately, though this is a subject of some contention, much of the consensus argues that the main strength of the hoplite phalanx was its utter inexorability when it operated as a cohesive, immaculately drilled unit – an unstoppable juggernaut which relied less on the initial clash of shield-walls (hoplites never advanced at a run, to preserve their formation) than on the relentless pushing force of their advance to shatter the enemy formation. Because only the first three ranks could bring their weapons to bear, the fight quickly degenerated into a shoving scrum until one side broke, which generally decided the outcome of the battle.

The Spartans, due to the ferocity of their training and the intensity of their drill, were peerless at phalanx warfare. They were Greece's only full-time soldiers, with most other cities fielding citizen militias instead, so they avoided the traditional hoplite problem of edging to the right, into the "shadow" of their rankmate's shield. This edging meant that undisciplined formations often found themselves outflanked, and all armies, including the Spartans, fielded their elite unit (in the Spartans' case the *hippeis*) to the far right to keep the line steady. The left was traditionally reserved for the *skiritai*, the Spartan rangers, who considered it their post of honor.

During the Persian Wars (499-449 BCE), hoplites proved their superiority against vastly larger Persian forces in battles like Marathon (490 BCE) Thermopylae (480 BCE) and Plataea (479 BCE). And when Alexander the Great crossed the Hellespont into Asia in 334 BCE and conquered the Persian Empire, the largest state of its time, it was largely thanks to the hoplites of the new and improved Macedonian phalanx. When Alexander's kingdom was divided among his generals, the militaries of his successor states largely relied on the Macedonian phalanx, effectively making hoplite warfare the standard throughout most of the known world.

It was only with the advent of the more mobile Roman legion, and the defeat of phalanxes in battles like Cynoscephalae (197 BCE) and Pydna (168 BCE), that the hoplite phalanx was finally outclassed, although not without a long fight: the last of Alexander's successor kingdoms, Ptolemaic Egypt, only fell in 31 BCE.

*Hoplites: The History and Legacy of the Ancient Greek Soldiers Who Revolutionized Infantry Warfare* examines how hoplites changed the world. Along with pictures depicting important people, places, and events, you will learn about hoplites like never before.

Hoplites: The History and Legacy of the Ancient Greek Soldiers Who Revolutionized Infantry Warfare

### Citizens, Soldiers, Patriots and Mercenaries

Throughout most of ancient Greek history, hoplites were not professional soldiers, but rather conscripted citizens fighting for their respective *poleis*, the hundreds of city-states, usually made up of a single fortified urban center and the surrounding countryside, into which ancient Greece was divided. These city-states formed the main political unit of the Greek civilization (Lee 2006: 480, 483; Hansen 2006: 1-3). However, this is not to say that ancient Greek hoplites were inexpert or untrained warriors: martial prowess was highly prized in ancient Greek society; it has been claimed the warfare was the main activity of the ancient Greek city-state (Quinn 2010). The strong ancient Greek athletic culture that created the Olympic Games was explicitly connected to training for war (Cornell 2002). Poleis like Athens, Thebes or Megara furthermore gave all their citizens basic military training, while fighting together with one's neighbors or fellow-citizens would increase unit cohesion (Lee: 483; Ray 2011: 9). In Classical Athens (by far the Greek *polis* for which historians have the most reliable sources), young men were enlisted in the military between the ages of 18 and 20, although they could be called to serve again as late as 60 (Aristotle, *Constitution of the Athenians*, 42).

Since ancient Greek soldiers were expected to provide their own gear, a soldier's role in battle was largely indicative of their social status (Lee: 481). In Athens, for example, the citizens were divided into political classes roughly equivalent to what gear they could provide in case of war (Aristotle, *Constitution of the Athenians*, 7). Generally, aristocrats served in the cavalry (Singor 2009: 593; Lee: 491; Roberts 2007: "*hippeis*"; Friend 2010).

Conversely, citizens too poor to afford a full hoplite panoply went into battle as lightly-armed *psiloi*, or else would serve as *thetes,* rowers or sailors in the navy--despite the image of ancient rowers as slaves, most of them were free men, and skilled sailors played a large role in the maintenance of naval supremacy for seafaring poleis like Athens (Roberts: "*thetes*") (for a first-hand account of Athenian pride in their own sailors, see for example Thucydides, *History of the Peloponnesian War,* I, 142-143).

The hoplites were generally made up of the "middle class" of the polis, largely landowning farmers, and they increased in importance as ancient Greek society advanced from the Dark Ages (1100-800BCE) into the Archaic Age (800-490 BCE). This transition from a more decentralized warfare centered on personal achievement and a largely aristocratic cavalry characteristic of the Dark Ages to the mass warfare that was characteristic of hoplites can be connected to the development of democracy, an invention of the Greek polis, and the increased political power of the middle classes—both compared to the old aristocracies, and to the lower classes who did not own any property (Lee: 485; Singor 490-495; Friend; Hanson 2000: 27; Cartledge 2013). The ancient Greek philosopher Aristotle already noticed the connection between political power and military service, linking cavalry to aristocratic forms of government, and the growth of infantry to the evolution of democracy in his *Politics* (Aristotle, *Politics*, IV, 3,

18).

Despite the fact that the hoplite citizen was the mainstay of warfare in the ancient Greek polis, as is perhaps natural in a world composed of hundreds of small cities constantly at war with each other, where every adult citizen is expected to know how to fight, certain men did make warfare a "full-time job". Thus, there were also a number of professional hoplites throughout the Greek poleis in the Archaic and Classical Greek eras, and many cities kept small units of select (*epilektoi*) soldiers who were paid by the state to train full-time. The most famous of these regiments was the "Sacred Band" of the polis of Thebes in the region of Boeotia, composed according to sources of pairs of homosexual lovers (Lee: 483).

The polis of Sparta was exceptional in ancient Greece in that its entire population was composed of soldiers, or (perhaps more accurately), in that its citizen body overlapped entirely with its hoplite force: all Spartan citizens were trained to be soldiers from a young age in the famously harsh *agoge* (Lee: 483-484). Sparta was consequently famous and feared for its military might throughout most of Greek history. All other work in the polis, including that of fighting as light infantry, was carried out by a subservient population known as *helots*, and the relatively freer *perioikoi* (Roberts: "*helot*" "*perioikoi*"). Spartan warfare was very focused on hoplites even when compared to other Greek cities. Beyond the light infantry being composed entirely of non-citizens, scholars know of no Spartan cavalry or navy in the recorded eras of their history until the final stages of the Peloponnesian War (431-404 BCE) (Connoly 2006: 40; Sekunda 1998: 7). According to an ancient saying, Sparta itself was unfortified, unlike other Greek cities, because its hoplites "were its walls." (Plutarch, *Moralia,* 217E).

**A 19<sup>th</sup> century illustration of a Hoplite**

Beyond trained citizen forces, because of their great skill in combat, Greek hoplites were also sought after as mercenaries both in and outside of Greece. Greek attitudes towards mercenaries were mixed, but it is indubitable that service abroad both existed and probably played a large role in the development of Greek warfare (Lee: 493-494; Hale 2013). The poet Alcaeus, from the polis of Mytilene, speaks proudly of the spoils collected by his brother when serving as a mercenary in Babylon (Alcaeus, fr. 350, 357). The poet Archilochus describes the experience of a mercenary hoplite succinctly: "The spear is my kneaded bread, the spear my Ismaric wine. On the spear I recline and drink." (Archilochus, fr. 2). In another poem (fr. 6), he muses about abandoning his shield in a distant land while fleeing battle.

One of the main historians from the Classical Era, Xenophon, was an Athenian who served as a mercenary alongside the Spartans. Among his many works there is a first-hand account of the march of a force of 10,000 Greeks deep into the Persian Empire while supporting the pretender to the Persian throne Cyrus the Younger (so named to distinguish him from the earlier Persian conqueror Cyrus the Great, of whom Xenophon also wrote a fictionalized biography). This is followed by the tale of their harrowing return to Greece through enemy territory after Cyrus's untimely death (Hale: 182; Xenophon, *Anabasis, Cyropaedia*).

A bust of Xenophon

**Men of Bronze**

Ancient amphora depicting phalanxes in combat

**A display case of armor used by hoplites**

"Nay, let each man close the foe, and with his own long spear, or else with his sword, wound and take an enemy, and setting foot beside foot, resting shield against shield, crest beside crest, helm beside helm, fight his man breast to breast with sword or long spear in hand." - - Tyrtaeus of Sparta, second half of the 7th century BCE (fr.8, lines 29-34)

The hoplite's main offensive weapon was the spear *(dory)*. It was around 2-2.5 meters (roughly 6.5-8.5 feet) in length, and about five centimeters (2 inches) wide, although in later time periods it became longer. The *dory* was usually made of ash or cornel wood, with an iron or bronze spearhead counterbalanced by a butt-spike that allowed it to be planted in the ground as well as continue to be used in combat even after breaking. The hoplite often carried a second spear, as depicted in both art and literature, which could be used either for throwing or as a spare. As a secondary weapon, the hoplite also carried a sword called a *xiphos*, and possibly also a dagger or knife (*encheireidion*) (Lee: 483; Hanson 2000: 83-88; Anderson 1995).

The hoplite's main defensive weapon was the *aspis* or *hoplon.* This was a large, heavy wooden shield, sometimes covered in bronze, or simply reinforced with a bronze rim. From archaeological evidence and reconstructions, we know it was at least three feet in diameter and half an inch thick, weighing about 16 pounds. It was usually handled with the left hand. An innovative part of the hoplite's shield was the double "Argive" grip (named after the city-state of Argos) which included both a handle (*antilabe*) and a supporting leather fastening (*porpax*), allowing for far easier handling than other shields of the time (Lee: 481-483; Viggiano, Van Wees 2013: 57-60; Hanson: 65-71; Anderson).

The hoplite shield was very important in the Greek conception of warfare: the alternative name for the shield, *hoplon*, also refers to the entirety of the hoplite panoply (panoply= "*pan hoplon*", lit. "all weapons"), and provided the term *hoplite* itself. The hoplite's shield was often decorated with various symbols, such as the apotropaic "gorgoneion", the head of the legendary monster Medusa, who turned men to stone with her gaze and was killed by Perseus before being placed on the shield of the goddess Athena (Potts 1982: 26-28). Sometimes, the symbols were personal, while other times, they were common to whole cities, such as the letters Mu for Messene, Sigma for Sicyon, the Club of Hercules for Thebes, the owl of Athena for Athens in later times, or, most famously, the Lambda on the Spartan shield, which stood for Lacedaemon or Laconia, alternative names for the city (Vaughn 1993: 54; Ray 2011: 10).

It has been traditionally stated that, because of the shape of the hoplite shield, each man would not be fully covered by his own shield, but could provide protection to the man to his left, and would in turn require protection from the man on his right: this would mean that the *aspis* could only be used to its full potential in a tight formation (Viggiano, Van Wees: 57-58; Hanson: 27-28). Whether or not this is true, it speaks to the strong link between the *aspis* and the war-culture of the ancient Greek hoplite, centered on fighting in solidarity with a group rather than individual heroics. Furthermore, the dead were traditionally carried from the battlefield on their shields, while abandoning one's shield, as seen in Archilochus, was tantamount to fleeing battle: this gave rise to the saying of the Spartan women to their sons when they went to battle "return with your shield or on it" (Plutarch, *Moralia,* 241F).

Almost as iconic as the *aspis* is the "Corinthian" helmet (named after the city-state of Corinth), which covered almost the entire face, thus offering a lot of protection but potentially limiting the hearing and range of vision of its wearer. In depictions, the Corinthian helmet usually features an imposing plumed crest (Hanson: 71-75; Viggiano, Van Wees 60-61). Another part of hoplite's armor was the heavy bronze corselet protecting the torso, and greaves, as well as arm- and thigh-guards (Viggiano, Van Wees: 61-63; Hanson: 76-83).

Given that it was particularly costly for the average ancient Greek citizen, hoplite armor and weaponry was often passed down in a family. Furthermore, although artistic depictions tend to show hoplites in full armor, it is not certain that every ancient Greek hoplite could afford the full kit: arm and thigh guards, for example, were relatively rare, and the widespread usage of the bronze corselet cannot be proven. And even the iconic Corinthian helmet may more often than not, especially in later times when hoplite armor grew progressively lighter, have given way to a less showy but also far less expensive leather cap called the *pilos* (Viggiano, Van Wees: 61-63; Hanson: 70).

It has traditionally been thought that the limitations of hoplite equipment severely impeded the way in which hoplites fought, essentially making hoplites slow, static warriors who were only fully efficient in a tight formation, the famous *phalanx*. However, while it is undeniable that the weaponry of the hoplite affected the way in which he fought, more recent theories have argued that these limitations are exaggerated, and that hoplite warfare was in fact far more flexible and fast paced than most people give it credit for.

The main battle formation in which the ancient hoplites fought was the phalanx, a densely packed formation about eight men deep, although in later years it got much deeper. The front rank of a phalanx formed a wall of shields, while the spears were held out forward, or, in the ranks behind, above the men in front of them in order to provide protection from enemy missiles. As mentioned earlier, each hoplite was covered not only by his own shield, but also by that of the man next to him, to such an extent that hoplite phalanxes tended to shift to the right as men instinctively sought cover (Lee: 483; Hanson: 85). This allegedly led to the traditional practice of placing the best soldiers on the right to hold the phalanx in place.

**An illustration depicting the phalanx formation**

Herodotus records the running charge of the Greeks against the Persians at the battle of Marathon as the first of its kind (Herodotus, *Histories*, VI, 112), implying furthermore that the advance of the hoplite phalanx was generally slow. One can thus imagine the terrifying scene of a marching hoplite phalanx as the slow and inexorable advance of a surface of spears and shields, creating a "killing zone" directly in front of it within range of the spears. Neither the missile weapons of the time, nor the relatively light cavalry that existed in Greece, were particularly efficient against a phalanx in proper formation, thus largely relegating these troops to supporting roles. The phalanx formation was, however, vulnerable to attacks from the flank and difficult to maneuver or even maintain on non-level terrain.

Since hoplite phalanxes were the main type of military unit in most Greek poleis, war was generally decided in confrontations between phalanxes. These were a highly ordered affair, with the armies aligning themselves opposite to each other on a level plain. After offering a sacrifice to the gods and singing the *paean*, a traditional victory hymn to the god Apollo, the opposing phalanxes would march against each other. A highly significant part of the confrontation was the *othismos* (literally "pushing"), in which the hoplites of the front rows would push against each other, supported by the men behind them, each trying to break the other side's shield wall. Once one of the phalanxes broke ranks, its hoplites, much weaker outside of formation, could be mowed down easily by their opponents who were still holding their shield wall. The breaking of a phalanx generally meant the end of the battle. After the battle, the winner would set up a trophy (*tropaion*) with the weaponry of their defeated enemies. The losing side would request the right to bury their dead. This was generally granted, not only because it was sacrilegious to refuse, but also because the request itself was an admission of defeat, and thus an end to hostilities (Lee: 484; Hanson: 27-30).

Traditionally, inter-polis hoplite warfare has been seen by scholars as almost a ritual shoving match between opposing phalanxes, with strict rules and limited casualties as the fight was generally accepted to be over once the ranks broke. However, more recently, scholars have begun to question the accuracy of such representations. Raising doubts about the practicality of *othismos* as a war tactic, and taking the term when used in ancient texts to more generally to refer to the ebb and flow of battle, scholars like Van Wees and Viggiano redefine our view of hoplite warfare, especially in the earlier days. They take their cues both from ancient artistic representations—such as vase paintings representing hoplites in a variety of different battle poses, or the poems of the Spartan Tyrtaeus describing different sorts of fighting activities and fighters, including *psiloi*, taking part in battle together—as well as the ways in which war is fought in modern-day primitive societies with weapons similar to those of the hoplites (albeit far lighter and more crude). Their argument is that hoplite warfare was in fact far more flexible and fast-paced than we give it credit for, with men continually running to and from the battle, reinforcing the front line, pelting and avoiding projectiles, and even resting in between bouts of fighting (Vigianno, Van Wees: 63-72; Lee: 485-486; Anderson: 15-16; Krentz 2013).

### The Archaic Era

Historically, traces of hoplite warfare can found as far back as the epics of Homer (approximately 8th century BCE), the oldest texts in the Greek, and, indeed, in Western canon. It is generally accepted that by the 7th century BCE hoplite warfare was the standard mode of fighting among the Greek poleis.

In a Greek world with literally hundreds of similar city-states, in which every citizen identified far more as, say, a Spartan or an Athenian than they did as a Greek, war was understandably very frequent. However, the scale of the wars of the Greek poleis was generally small. Wars were fought over territory, raids, or old rivalries between poleis, and it was rare for several poleis band together in an alliance. The standard procedure for a war was for the hoplites of two opposing poleis to meet on a level field and fight each other in an orderly phalanx battle.

As most of the armies fighting were similar, rules and traditions, like the taboo against forbidding the burial of the dead to the defeated army, or the Olympic truce, which enforced a peace every four years for the duration of the Olympic Games (the earliest games are recorded in 776 BCE), controlled both the scope and method of this constant warfare. Furthermore, it was very rare that a hoplite expedition would last more than a single season. After all, the forces of citizen-soldiers on both sides were needed at home to tend to their farms and businesses, and it was to the interest of the both of the opposing armies to decide the war within a time limit, largely avoiding skirmishes or guerilla warfare. It was also very rare for any polis to annex another, so once a hoplite force forfeited the field and fell back behind the walls of its polis, or to its city's citadel (*acropolis*), a protracted siege was very impractical, and the integrity of any single polis as a political entity was thus generally guaranteed—besides, seeing things from the attacker's perspective, it is would be very difficult for a city-state to integrate a conquered polis, and to expand beyond one city and still be a city-state. This state of affairs, however, also meant that the rivalries and conflicts between poleis often went unresolved for several decades (Singor; Hanson: 27-39).

Written sources about specific wars in the Archaic Era are scanty. Examples of conflicts in this time period include the rivalry between the poleis Sparta and Argos and the protracted fight between Athens and Megara over the island of Salamis (Hanson: 597-599). Another example is the Lelantine War, a rivalry over the fertile Lelantine Plain on the island of Euboea between the two poleis of Chalchis and Eretria. The Lelantine War was fought in several phases over 70 years, leaving a strong impression on contemporary poets and later historians. However, as the historian Herodotus informs readers, this was an atypical war for the time; according to him, it was the first time in Greek history both sides in a war received support from other poleis (Williams 2010; Herodotus, V, 99; Plutarch, *Moralia*, 153f-154a; Thucydides, I, 15).

Another atypical example of archaic war is the Messenian War, fought between the poleis of Messene and Sparta: although it began traditionally enough, with a raid by one side on a temple near the border during a religious festival (the accounts of "who started it" vary between the Spartans and the Messenians), it took on a far greater scale, and only ended after many years and a protracted siege. The result was a full annexation of Messene and the surrounding region, and the subjugation of Messene's citizens into Spartan *helots* (Pausanias, *Description of Greece* IV, 9-13). This Messenian war was also crucial to the militaristic development of Sparta, as not only did the control of the fertile Messenian plain and the enslaved population of Messene give Sparta the resources to dedicate all their citizen population to professional warfare, but the constant threat of Messenian revolt, and the need to control their now atypically large territory and subservient population, gave them a very good incentive to do this (Nafissi 2009: 120-123; Cartledge 2010).

During the Archaic Period, hoplite-style warfare also expanded beyond the confines of Greece in what is known as the Greek colonization (*apoikismos*). The population of Greece grew, and because of their confined geographical situation, the city-states sent off expeditions to found new poleis in distant lands. Unlike later colonies of other civilizations, these poleis were more or less independent from their mother-cities, only connected to them by religious and commercial ties. Greek poleis were founded throughout the Mediterranean and Black Seas, in places as diverse as Asia Minor, Libya, Egypt, Crimea, Southern Italy, Spain and modern-day France; and with them, hoplite warfare spread throughout these areas.

Sources regarding the warfare of these poleis is even more scanty than what exists for those of mainland Greece, but their hoplites were presumably successful, as these new city-states managed to survive and thrive not only against the local natives but also against other Mediterranean powers, such as the Phoenicians, who many times competed with the Greeks during colonization (Antonacci 2009; Tsekhaladze 2009). It is certainly known from archaeological finds that many local populations adopted elements of Greek culture, including hoplite-style warfare, in particular the Etruscans and other native populations of Italy, as well as the then-small native city-state of Rome. Rome would in time develop its warfare far beyond what the first Greeks to arrive in Italy would have imagined.

The size and scale of hoplite conflicts in the Archaic Era, however, would pale in comparison to the foreign foe Greek hoplites would face in the subsequent Classical Era.

**The Persian Wars**

During the 6th century BCE, the Persians (also referred to in Greek sources as the "Medes") broke out of their heartland in modern-day Iran and began an unprecedented series of conquests throughout the Middle East. Under leaders like Cyrus the Great and Cambyses, the Persian Empire toppled ancient kingdoms, and took control of areas as diverse and vast as Babylon, Egypt, Syria, Israel and Asia Minor. By the end of the century, the Persian monarch, known as the "King of Kings", or in Greek simply the "Great King" (*megas basileus*), ruled what at the time was the largest empire in human history.

**A bust of Cyrus the Great**

The Persian way of fighting, to a degree in line with that of earlier Middle Eastern empires like Assyria, was very different to that of the Greeks: Persians relied on heavy noble cavalry and organized units of archers. The efficiency of this style of fighting, especially of heavy cavalry, would prove dubious in the fragmented and mountainous terrain of Greece, filled with narrow valleys and small plains. Furthermore, the Persian army was recruited from a vast, multi-ethnic empire fighting under a single king, while the Greeks were generally organized in more egalitarian, homogenous armies of free men fighting for their specific poleis (Raaflaub 2013).

During their conquests, the Persians had also subdued some of the Greek poleis on the coast of Asia Minor, an area known as Ionia because of the specific tribe of Greeks that had colonized it. In 499BCE, these poleis revolted against the Persians. When the Greek city-states of Athens and Eretria sent them support, this was seen as a direct challenge to the Persian king Darius, and ultimately embroiled the entirety of Greece in a conflict with Persia (Herodotus, *Histories*, V, 35-VI, 33). The war with Persia would be on a scale far greater than anything the Greek poleis had faced before, and it would both prove the worth of hoplite warfare and affect its future development.

The story of Persia's ascendancy and of the conflict against the Greek city-states is recorded in what is widely considered to be the earliest known historical work, Herodotus's *Histories* (the term in Greek means simply "inquiry"). After re-subjugating Ionia in 492 BCE, Darius sent envoys to the main Greek city-states, including Sparta and Athens, demanding tokens of earth and water as symbols of submission. Darius didn't exactly get the answer he was looking for. According to Herodotus in his famous *Histories*, "Xerxes however had not sent to Athens or to Sparta heralds to demand the gift of earth, and for this reason, namely because at the former time when Dareios had sent for this very purpose, the one people threw the men who made the demand into the pit and the others into a well, and bade them take from thence earth and water and bear them to the king."

Thus, Darius initiated a campaign to subjugate Greece (Herodotus, VI, 48-49) (Holland: 178-179). After subduing Thrace and Macedon in the north with a first expedition (Herodotus, VI, 43-46), the Persians sent a second expedition by sea across the Aegean. This expedition violently conquered several islands along the way, including Euboea, on which the polis of Eretria was situated (Herodotus, VI, 94-101). The Persians then disembarked in mainland Greece near the plain of Marathon, about 42 km (26 miles) from Athens, where they would fight the hoplite army of the Athenian polis (Herodotus, VI, 102). This was the first place where the Persians met significant resistance. According to the historian Herodotus, the Athenians at Marathon were the "[f]irst to endure looking at Median dress and men wearing it, for up until then just hearing the name of the Medes caused the Hellenes [Greeks] to panic." (Herodotus, VI, 112).

**Ancient Greek depiction of the Persian Emperor Darius**

The Persian army, numbering anywhere between 30,000 and 300,000 men, landed on the plain at Marathon, a few dozen miles from Athens, where an Athenian army of 10,000 hoplite heavy infantry supported by 1,000 Plataeans prepared to contest their passage. The Athenians appealed to the Spartans for help, but the Spartans dithered; according to the Laws of Lycurgus, they were forbidden to march until the waxing moon was full. Accordingly, their army arrived too late. Thus, it fell upon the Athenians to shoulder the burden.

At Marathon, the until-then undefeated Persians were met by the Athenian general Miltiades (Herodotus, VI, 103) and the entirety of Athens' citizen hoplite force (Holland 2006: 187-190). Coming out to meet the Persians incurred a great risk on part of the Athenians: although the Athenian army was still vastly outnumbered (figures are not given by Herodotus, but the estimates of later ancient sources range from 200,000 to 600, 000 for the Persian side),[1] they had also left Athens proper completely defenceless: a defeat would spell a complete destruction for

---

[1] Cornelius Nepos, *Life of Miltiades*, V; Pausanias, *Description of Greece*, X, 22; Plutarch, *Moralia*, 305B; Justin, *History*, II, 9; Lysias, *Funeral Oration*, 21; Plato, *Menexenus*, 240A.

their polis.

Miltiades' first move was to take advantage of the terrain by blocking all the issues from the plain of Marathon with his heavy infantry (Cornelius Nepos, *Life of Miltiades*, IV). This positioning was followed by a stalemate, although Herodotus himself is not clear as to why the attack was delayed or what spurred the Greeks to attack when they did: it is theorized that Miltiades attacked when the Persians decided to embark their best troops, the heavy cavalry, and head straight for Athens (Holland: 187-190). It was only after several days that. Miltiades attacked the Persians on the coast (Herodotus, VI, 109-111). According to Herodotus, this was the first time Greek hoplites had charged at an enemy at a run (Herodotus, V, 112); this is likely because it was the first time they met with an enemy force using primarily long-ranged weapons (Lazenby 1993: 66-69).

However, the hail of Persian arrows proved incapable of penetrating the hoplites' heavy shields and armor; and rather than proving easy picking for the Persian archers, as the Persians had expected (Herodotus says that they thought that the Greeks were mad for charging them head on) the much more heavily armed hoplites fell on the Persian troops largely intact, and inflicted a crushing defeat (Herodotus, VI, 112-114). According to Herodotus, there were 6,400 casualties for the Persians, 192 for the Athenians and 11 for the Plataeans (Herodotus, VI, 117).

According to legend, in the aftermath of Marathon one of the Greek soldiers, already battle-weary, named Pheidippides, ran the 26.2 miles back to Athens in order to announce the victory and collapsed and died as soon as he had done so, leading to the establishment of the marathon in memory of that feat in the modern Olympics. The battle has another, less inspiring aftermath, however. The year after Marathon, in 489 B.C., an expedition under Miltiades was launched against the Greek traitors at Paros. The expedition was a failure and, in what would become one of Athens's less charming traditions, the hero of the hour was turned into the villain by demagogues who realized the power of an inflamed mob in the new democratic system; Miltiades, wounded and suffering, was sentenced to death and thrown into prison, where he died of his wounds.

**Tilemahos Efthimiadis's picture of an Athenian soldier's uniform**

This was the Persians' first defeat on Greek soil, and in addition to demonstrating that Persians could be defeated, it also showcased the advantages of hoplite armies against the Persian style of warfare. After a failed attempt at landing in Athens proper (Herodotus, VI, 115-116), the Persian expedition force retreated. King Darius immediately began to raise a massive army to retaliate, but internal conflict in the Persian Empire, set off by a revolt in Egypt, prevented him from carrying out his plans (Herodotus, VII, 1-5). Thus, the second invasion of Greece would be undertaken by his son Xerxes.

Herodotus reports the second Persian invasion force as having been several million men strong (Herodotus, VII, 185). While this is generally agreed by modern scholars to be a wild exaggeration, the more conservative 120,000-300,000 that historians agree on (Holland: 394) is still very impressive for any state at that point in history. Xerxes had furthermore secured the either tacitly or openly expressed promise of submission and support upon arrival from several Greek states and powerful families (Herodotus, VII, 6-10, 150). Nonetheless, in 481 BCE, representatives from many of the most powerful poleis, notably Sparta and Athens, met at Corinth and swore and alliance to fight the Persians (Herodotus, VII, 145-160). This was one of the first Pan-Hellenic (Greece-wide) alliances against a common foe, and a remarkable occurrence for its time, especially considering that many of the states in the alliance had been or even were at war with each other (Holland: 226).

After crossing from Asia to Europe on pontoon bridges (a remarkable feat of engineering) (Herodotus, VII, 35-37), the Persians again came down through Thrace and Macedon, largely unopposed. The Greeks' first plan was to meet the Persians at the valley of Tempe (Herodotus, VII, 173), blocking Persian advance with their heavy infantry. This would force the Persians to squeeze through a narrow pass in limited numbers, making their vast numerical advantage meaningless against the more heavily armed hoplites. However, upon finding that the valley could be bypassed, the Greeks fell back and decided instead to fight the Persians at the narrow pass of Thermopylae further south. They would also prevent the advance of the attached Persian fleet by blocking the straits at Artemisium with their combined navies, the most significant of which was that of Athens (Herodotus, VIII, 1-2, 175-177).

**A modern view of the pass at Thermopylae. At the time of the battle, the coastline was roughly where the road is today, and the trees on the left side of the picture would most likely have not been there.**

Because the battle of Thermopylae (480 BCE) occurred at the time of a double sacred truce, coinciding with the *Carneia* festival and the Olympic Games, the Spartans were again of the opinion that it would be sacrilegious to dispatch a large force (Herodotus, VII, 206), and finally decided to only send 300 elite troops under their king Leonidas (Herodotus, VII, 205). Interestingly, and perhaps a throwback by the very traditional Spartans to the era before hoplite warfare, these elite troops were called *hippeis*, or "knights", despite being infantry rather than cavalry (Wheeler 1993: 131); however, the body of young warriors that typically made up the Spartan *hippeis* had been replaced by older fighters with living sons to ensure that their bloodlines could be continued if they fell in battle. Despite the iconic view of Thermopylae as the last stand of the 300 Spartans, the Spartans were in fact holding out for the end of the Olympic truce to send a larger force, and were furthermore reinforced along the way by several other Greek city-states, their army amounting to about 7000 troops by the time they reached Thermopylae in August of 480 BCE (Herodotus, VII, 202).

The Greeks held off the Persians at Thermopylae for several days. However, eventually, the Persian forces managed to find a path to outflank the Greeks; only then did the majority of the Greek force decide to fall back, and it was at this point that the Spartans resolved to make their famous last stand, along with some Thespian allies (Herodotus, VII, 210-227). The exact reasoning for this is dubious, but it was most probably in order to cover the retreat of the other Greeks (Lazenby: 144-145; Holland: 294): retreating hoplites out of formation would be easy picking for the much faster heavy Persian cavalry.

In the aftermath of Thermopylae, Xerxes would subdue a large part of Greece north of the Isthmus of Corinth (the narrow stretch of land that united the landmass known as the Peloponnese in the south with the rest of mainland Greece); however, his fleet was defeated twice at Artemisium (Herodotus, VIII, 10-22) and again at Salamis (Herodotus, VIII, 83-97), the island where the Athenians had ended up falling back after their mainland city was taken. This latter battle was particularly significant, as it decimated the Persian fleet. After being offered favorable surrender terms by the Persians, which they refused, the allied poleis as a whole decided to continue the war. The Spartans were again being delayed, this time the *Hyacinthia* festival. But upon being delivered an ultimatum by the poleis of Athens, Megara and Plataea that the Persian terms would be accepted if Sparta did not send troops, they eventually came in full force (Herodotus, IX, 7-11), marshalling perhaps the largest army of hoplites Sparta had ever assembled (Holland: 343-349).

The allied Greek poleis met the Persian army and its Greek allies at Plataea. According to ancient sources the Greek force was around 100,000 men strong (Herodotus, IX, 28-29;

Diodorus Siculus, *Library of History*, IX, 30.1), while the Persians are reported at having been anywhere from 350,000-500,000 men strong (Herodotus, IX, 32; Diodorus Siculus, IX, 30.1). Modern estimates place the numbers closer to 80,000 Greeks and 150,000-250,000 Persians) (Holland: 400; Lazenby: 227-228). The battle, much like Marathon, began as a stalemate. However when the Persians attacked the Greek supply lines to weaken their stand, the Greeks decided to fall back and defend them (Herodotus, IX, 51-52). Thinking their opponents were retreating, the Persians began to chase them and broke ranks (Herodotus, IX, 58-59). At that point, the Greeks met them in an orderly fashion, and the phalanx again carried the day (Herodotus, IX, 60-70). The simultaneous naval battle of Mycale destroyed the remnants of the Persian fleet, and marked the end of Persian military presence in mainland Greece (Herodotus, IX, 96-100).

The Persian Wars were a turning point in military history for Greece. On the one hand, the war tactics of the Greek city-states, especially the hoplite phalanx, proved roundly superior, despite a numerical disadvantage, to the army of the largest empire of their day, which had until then been a more-or-less unstoppable conquering war machine. This was also arguably when the Greeks began to view themselves as sharing a Hellenic identity rather than being simply citizens of their respective poleis. It also reinforced the idea, in the Greek mindset, of Greek freedom as opposed to foreign tyranny.

On the other hand, the Persian Wars also challenged many traditional notions of hoplite warfare. Facing a much larger foe, the Greek poleis were forced to join in alliances and fight much more protracted wars on a far larger scale than they were used to, while the religious and traditional constraints on warfare, such as the Olympic truce, proved to be impractical outside of the almost ritualistic confines of inter-polis warfare. These changes would be exacerbated in later years, and would reach their culmination in the Peloponnesian War, a far less glorious affair which would strain traditional hoplite warfare beyond its breaking point.

### The Peloponnesian War and its Aftermath

In the aftermath of the Persian Wars in mainland Greece, the Greek city-states experienced a golden age of expansion and prosperity, and also of newfound ambition. Sparta was evidently still conflicted about pursuing expansionism outside of the Peloponnese and Greece itself. Thus, they turned down overtures from the Ionian cities for help in their renewed revolt against Xerxes, rudely suggesting that they abandon their cities *en masse* and resettle in Greece, where space would be made for them by uprooting pro-Persian traitors. The Ionians, disgusted, refused to support Pausanias (now in the role of *navarch*, or admiral) in his expeditions against Byzantium and Cyprus and instead turned to Athens for help, which the seafaring power was pleased to provide. The seeds of Athenian and Spartan rivalry, seeds which would eventually blossom into the worst war in Greece's history, had been sown.

The Athenians, by contrast, were thinking bigger. Over the following decade they spearheaded a number of naval actions against Persian-held settlements and fortresses in the Aegean, further expanding Athens's influence and laying the basis for what would later become the Athenian empire. During this period the Athenian fleet, already pre-eminent, expanded and grew in experience and ability until it was the most powerful naval force in all of the Mediterranean.

It was during this period that Athens established the Delian League; initially envisioned as a league of like-minded *poleis* with Athens acting as first among equals, but it quickly degenerated into a situation where other cities were essentially vassals of Athens. Meanwhile, the Spartans had begun to grow increasingly concerned about Athens's imperialistic ambitions and worried that their position of pre-eminence among the Greeks would soon be subverted. A crisis, it seemed, was inevitable.

Athens would continue the Persian Wars by launching many expeditions against Persian interests in Europe as well as Asia and Africa, fighting the Persians in places like Thrace, Cyprus and Asia Minor (Thucydides, I, 98-100), and even sending a large contingent of hoplite warriors to support a rebellion against the Persians in Egypt (Thucydides, *Histories*, I, 104, 109-110). Athens also began to assert dominance over the other Greek city-states, particularly those of Ionia and the Aegean islands.

At the same time, however, a wedge was being driven between Athens and other powerful city-states, including Thebes and Corinth, and especially Sparta, as the other major poleis were growing weary of Athenian attempts at dominance in Greek politics. The culmination of these developments was the removal of the treasury of the Delian League from Delos to Athens, effectively resulting in Athens taking full control of the League's finances and turning the erstwhile defensive alliance into an Athenian Empire (Thucydides, I, 18-19) (Brock 2006; Welwei 2006: 526-528; Roberts "Delian League").

Under the leadership of Pericles, the great statesman who took power in Athens in 461 BCE and held it largely without interruption until his death 30 years later, the city flourished culturally. The arts, including theater, poetry and philosophy, blossomed like in no other city in Greece, as did science, including architecture, medicine, natural philosophy and mathematics. Athens could boast, and with good cause, that all of Greece looked to them for its knowledge, but there was trouble in paradise. The dynamism and expansion hid the reality of oppression of other fellow members of the Delian League, whose lavish tribute was needed to fund Athens's public works and its various schools. Many of the Delian allies were resentful, and the Spartans were downright hostile. And throughout it all, the politicians of Athens relentlessly schemed and betrayed each other in a constant quest for power and influence. A crisis was coming, but Athens rushed blissfully unaware towards it. Indeed, there is even some indication that Pericles deliberately orchestrated it to preserve himself from political issues at home.

**Bust of Pericles**

    After several decades of escalating tensions, in 431 BCE war eventually broke out between Sparta and its allies on one side, and Athens and its allies on the other. The protracted and devastating conflict that ensued would span almost three decades of total war, involving most of the major city-states in Greece as well as foreign powers. Thucydides, the historian of this "Peloponnesian War" (so named because Sparta and many of its allies, notably Corinth, were located on the Peloponnese), picked up Greek history largely where Herodotus left off, albeit with an impressively more rationalistic outlook on events. He does not fail to notice the transformation in the modes of warfare, the unprecedented scale of the Peloponnesian War, or the devastation it caused when compared to the wars of previous epochs (Thucydides, I, 1, 23). Tellingly, if perhaps with some exaggeration, Thucydides calls the Peloponnesian War the greatest war to ever occur, "for Greeks and barbarians [non-Greeks] alike".

As it soon became clear that the Spartans would dominate on land and the Athenians at sea, the war quickly devolved into a deadly stalemate in which the Athenians, besieged behind their "Long Walls" (a massive fortification hastily constructed in the buildup to the war, which connected Athens proper with its port-city in Piraeus) (Thucydides I 89-93), nonetheless kept control of the sea and launched several raids and expeditions against the Peloponnesians. The Athenian strategy, as expressed by Pericles (Thucydides I, 140-144, II, 35-46), consisted in making Athens into a "land-island", and winning the war by attrition.

That said, several attempts were made by either side to gain the upper hand, notably the Sicilian Expedition on part of Athens in 415-413 BCE. The Sicilian expedition was an attempt to subdue the rich city-state of Syracuse in southern Italy, a distant ally of Sparta, but it ultimately ended in an unmitigated disaster for the Athenians, severely depleting their morale and manpower and spurring several violent revolts from their allies (Thucydides, VI-VIII).

Throughout the war, both sides had been particularly hostile to any poleis either leaving or not joining either of their alliances, and several city-states who wished to remain neutral were forced to pick sides. A particular example on which Thucydides dwells is the small island polis of Melos, which was utterly destroyed by the Athenians after attempting to remain neutral (Thucydides, V, 84-116).

The Peloponnesian War concluded long after the death of Pericles, and presumably also of Thucydides, who did not finish his work. According to the historian and mercenary commander Xenophon, who amongst his other works also wrote the *Hellenica* ("Affairs of the Greeks"), a continuation of Thucydides's history, the war was brought to an end with help from the Persians, who perceived the Athenians as a far more direct threat to their interests than the Spartans. With Persian gold, the Spartans acquired a navy and, after a series of battles, managed to cut off besieged Athens' naval supply line of grain from its allied poleis in the Black Sea (Xenophon, *Hellenica*, I, 4-6, II, 1-2; the alliance between the Persians and Sparta does, however, first show up in Thucydides in book VIII, chapter 37). In addition to a navy, the Spartans also began to add actual cavalry detachments to their until-then exclusively infantry-based armies (Connolly: 40).

In 404 BCE, Athens was finally forced to surrender, submitting to a pro-Spartan government and tearing down its Long Walls (Xenophon *Hellenica*, II, 2) (Tritle 2010) (Welwei: 528-535). In the aftermath of the war, and in line with their Persian alliance, Sparta also got involved, unsuccessfully, in internal Persian politics, supporting the rebellion of the then-Persian king's brother Cyrus the Younger, as chronicled in Xenophon's *Anabasis*.

While Sparta won the Peloponnesian War, it was almost as ruined as all the other Greek poleis. Furthermore, because its main promise had been freedom from Athenian dominance, and also simply from a sheer lack of manpower, in the following decades Sparta found it difficult to assert any sort of lasting authority over the other poleis, both the former allies of Athens and their own, even if they attempted to do so by establishing garrisons in other city-states and reaching various agreements with the Persians. A particularly severe blow to the Spartans was the defeat of a *mora*, a regiment of Spartan hoplites, which was annihilated by a troop of lightly-armed *peltasts* under the Athenian general Iphicrates in 392 BCE (Welwei: 535-537).

It was this state of things, with the Greek city-states still striving to assert or acquire dominance in the wake of the Peloponnesian War, that led to the short-lived supremacy of Sparta's erstwhile ally Thebes in Greek affairs, known at the Theban hegemony. After a revolt against a puppet government installed by Sparta, the Thebans established dominance by defeating the powerful (and numerically superior) Spartans at the battle of Leuctra in 371 BCE. Thebes' ascendancy was due in no small part to the leadership and tactical innovations of their general Epaminondas, which included longer spears and the use of a wedge formation, and which allowed them to largely outclass the hoplite phalanxes of all the other city-states. At Leuctra in particular, aware that he could not efficiently match the size of the more numerous Spartan phalanx, Epaminondas set up his own phalanx 50 men deep opposite to the strongest section of the Spartan army. Contrary to Greek custom of placing the better warriors on the right, Epaminondas placed himself and the elite Theban "Sacred Band" on the far left, directly opposite the top Spartan troops, while directing the troops on the right (the Spartan left) to offer no resistance to their opponents.

Outnumbered, Epaminondas was counting on breaking the Spartan army by defeating their elite troops, and unusually for a Greek battle, Leuctra opened with a mutual cavalry charge, in which the Thebans soundly defeated the Spartans. The old-fashioned, traditionally aristocratic Thebans (although Epaminondas himself was a democrat), whose polis was located on the plain of Boeotia, specialized in cavalry in comparison to the rest of Greeks (this may be what led to their affinity with the Persians during the Persian Wars, a connection which they never lived down). The retreating Spartan cavalry was especially troublesome, as it caused problems for the Spartan phalanx. The opening clash was followed by a march, at double speed, by Epaminondas and his best troops directly against the Spartan elite, led by the Spartan king Cleombrotus in person. The deeper Theban phalanx carried the day, and Cleombrotus died on the battlefield. When their elite right wing broke ranks, the rest of the Spartan army and its allies retreated, and the Thebans won the battle (Xenophon, *Hellenica* VI 4, 6-15) (Welwei: 537-541).

The Theban hegemony after Leuctra was particularly short-lived, although it crippled Spartan dominance and also largely allowed Athens to recover its status as a Greek power by rapidly rebuilding at least the core of its former empire of seafaring poleis. In particular, the Thebans secured independence for the city-state of Messene, whose inhabitants had been Spartan helots for several centuries (Diodorus Siculus, *Historic Library*, XV, 66), thus dealing a severe and permanent blow to the Spartan military apparatus. Theban hegemony, for its part, ended more or less with the death of Epaminondas, after which the Theban forces were defeated by Spartans and their allies at Mantinea in the Peloponnese (Xenophon, *Hellenica*, VII, 5, 21-27) (LaForse 2006: 544-551).

As the aftermath made clear, the Peloponnesian War, beyond its sheer scale, was also transformative for both the nature of hoplite warfare and ancient Greek politics in general. Rather than largely autonomous poleis, Greece was now organized as a network of alliances led by larger city-states vying for supremacy, and often violently imposing their dominance on smaller "allies". Furthermore, although they had been defeated militarily in the Persian Wars, the alliance between Sparta and Persia paved the way for Persian intervention in Greek internal affairs, which continued throughout the following century. The Persians continued playing arbiter in inter-polis relations, notably, for example, with the famous "King's Peace" of 387 BCE (Welwei). On the field of battle, innovative tactics such as those of Epaminondas proved that hoplite warfare could be versatile and adapt new, more effective strategies. At the same time, however, aspects of traditional warfare, like the Olympic truce or the simple fact of returning home after a short expedition, were proven obsolete by events like the Spartan siege of Athens, and the defeat of a Spartan phalanx by a force composed largely of light infantry cast doubt on the very supremacy of the hoplite on the Greek battlefield.

Many of these developments paved the way, in less than a century, for the even more momentous changes under King Philip of Macedon and his legendary son Alexander the Great.

### The Macedonians

"How great are the dangers I face to win a good name in Athens." – Alexander the Great

Located on the northern fringe of the Greek world, the kingdom of Macedon had for most of history played a secondary role in the politics of the richer and more powerful poleis to the south. This would change with the ascension of Philip II to the throne. Having been a political hostage in Thebes for much of his youth, Philip had studied under Epaminondas in Thebes (Diodorus Siculus, XVI, 2), and perhaps his most significant contribution to war history was the completion of the revolutionizing of hoplite warfare begun by the latter (LaForse: 552-555).

The main development to the Macedonian phalanx under Philip was the drilling of his hoplites as a professional force (Errington 1990: 238, 247) and the equipment of his hoplites with the *sarissa*, a weapon much longer than the traditional hoplite spear, reaching an impressive 5 or 6 meters in length (16-20 feet). The sarissa was in fact so long it was normally transported in two parts and assembled before battle. Although the Macedonian phalanx was less effective at forming a shield wall than traditional phalanxes, thanks to the sarissa, men as far as 5 ranks deep in the phalanx could participate in the front line of the battle, further increasing the efficiency of the phalanx's "killing zone", and proving just as effective, if not more, at dealing with another phalanx's shield wall. According to the historian Polybius, a single man coming up against the Macedonian phalanx would have to deal with approximately ten spear points simultaneously, making a frontal attack against the formation all but impossible. The Macedonian phalanx was also more manoeuvrable than its more traditional counterpart: in general, the Macedonian phalangite had lighter weapons than the traditional hoplite, and thus a much faster marching speed than most armies of the time (Polybius, *Histories*, 28-32) (Connolly: 68-69) (LaForse: 555).

Furthermore, Philip's military strategy did not rely solely, or even primarily, on the phalanx: its weak flanks were defended by lighter troops like *peltastes* (Ashley 2004: 45-46), and he made use of the cavalry as a striking force, especially the elite heavy *hetairoi,* or "Companion" cavalry: Macedon, like Thebes, was uncharacteristically flat compared to southern Greece, and had a strong cavalry tradition. Philip furthermore used an engineer corps and began to extensively adopt siege engines like battering rams and siege towers (LaForse: 555). The development of efficient siege warfare reduced the impregnability of cities at a time when, very often, war could be brought to a standstill by one side simply retreating behind its walls (as happened with Athens during the Peloponnesian War). Although somewhat understated in mainland Greece, this would have contributed to making the polis far less effective as a political and military unit.

**A bust of Philip**

  Throughout his reign, Philip expanded his influence in Greece, involving himself in several wars between poleis. By simultaneously expanding his dominions to the north outside of Greece, he eventually made his once-marginal kingdom the main player in Greek politics, causing great tension between himself and the more powerful city-states (Diodorus Siculus, XVI). The view on Philip in the poleis varies widely: many Greeks were willing to see him as a unifier of Greece and the man to bring peace and an end to the seemingly interminable conflicts between the warring leagues of city-states. This is the view preserved by the speeches of the contemporary Athenian orators Aeschines and, in his later years, Isocrates. Other Greeks, notably the Athenian orator Demosthenes, decried Philip as not Greek at all, but a foreign "barbarian" invader like Xerxes had been during the Persian Wars (LaForse: 552-556).

Things came to a head when, at the behest of Demosthenes and against the terms of a previous peace treaty between the two, the Athenians sent aid to Byzantium, a city which Philip was besieging. As retaliation, Philip marched south. His son, Alexander, was also commanding a portion of his army (Cawkwell 1978: 118-140). The Athenians, along with an alliance of other city-states, (most notably their former enemy Thebes), met Philip's troops at Chaeronea (Diodorus Siculus, XVI, 77, 84-85). Despite having the better ground, both flanks of the Theban-Athenian army were broken, and the whole army was routed (Diodorus Siculus, XVI, 86), with only the Theban Sacred Band, which had until then been undefeated, holding their ground (Plutarch, *Life of Pelopidas,* 18; *Life of Alexander* 9). After the battle, which demonstrated the superiority of the Macedonian army to the traditional phalanx of the poleis, Philip had control of the whole of Greece. In 337 BCE he founded the League of Corinth, a new coalition of Greek states with himself as leader. Out of the major Greek city-states only Sparta remained neutral (Cawkwell: 148-179). In 336 BCE, Philip was assassinated during a religious festival, but his son Alexander promptly took control of his kingdom; and after rapidly subduing an attempted revolt from the poleis and securing Macedon's northern border, Alexander set his sights on Persia (La Forse: 556-558).

Alexander crossed the Hellespont into Persian territory in 334 BCE with an army of 12,000 Macedonian hoplites, 7,000 allies from the poleis, 5,000 mercenaries, and 7,000 light infantry, as well as at least 5,000 cavalry. A tactical genius, Alexander's campaign would be the stuff of legends. He brought further innovations to warfare, further eschewing reliance of the phalanx in favour of combined arms tactics. Alexander's favored use for the phalanx was pinning down his enemies, especially for attacks by his Companion cavalry (Ashley: 39), while many of his victories would include large-scale siege warfare. In Persia, Alexander was first met by Memnon of Rhodes, a Greek mercenary commander, and various Persian provincial governors (*satraps)*. These he defeated at the battle of the Granicus River, using feints and combined cavalry and infantry tactics.[2] After his victory, Alexander dedicated a trophy to himself and all the Greeks "except the Lacedemonians [Spartans]" (Heckel 2006: 563-564).

---

[2] The ancient accounts of the specifics of this battle, mainly the historians Arrian and Diodorus Siculus, vary widely.

**Andrew Dunn's picture of a bust of Alexander**

Alexander subsequently continued his campaign in Asia Minor, establishing Greek-style democracies in several cities. A major blow was delivered to the Persians when he besieged and took the city of Halicarnassus, an important base for the Persian navy (Heckel: 564-565). After the death of Memnon and the execution of his successor, the Athenian Karademas, the king of Persia Darius III personally took control of the Persian army. Alexander met Darius at Issus in 333 BCE, once again on a river bank (on the Pinarus River), thus minimizing the Persian king's numerical advantage. During the battle, Alexander used his mobile elite cavalry as shock troops, routing several points of the Persian army, as well as Persian war chariots under Darius himself, and personally chasing the Persian king from the field (Heckel: 565). After this, Alexander proceeded to besiege and take several key Persian cities, including Tyre and Gaza (Heckel: 566-567), before advancing to the east and decisively defeating the Persians at Gaugamela in 331 BCE (Heckel: 567-569).

After completing the conquest of Persia, including a personal manhunt against Darius and the defeat of his last loyal satraps, Alexander marched into India, but despite initial success (including at the battle of the Hydaspes, where the heavily outnumbered Macedonian phalanx managed to route not only Indian infantry and cavalry, but even war elephants), Alexander eventually returned west, with his army tired of campaigning (Heckel: 577-579).

Alexander died soon after in Babylon in 323 BCE, and his empire was divided among his generals (Heckel: 581) (Holt 2010). However, his conquests had paved the way for the new (and final) phase in the history of hoplite warfare.

### The End of the Hoplite Era

After the death of Alexander, several powerful kingdoms rose in the wake of his empire. These states, who would dominate history in the area for approximately the next three centuries, were ruled by Alexander's generals and their successors. They are known as Hellenistic, or "Greek-like", because although run by Greek dynasties, they combined Greek and non-Greek cultures and populations. At the same time, the old polis city-states largely regained their independence to a greater or lesser extent, organizing themselves into various leagues to defend their interests against the much larger kingdoms; mainland Greece would, however, never again be the center of the Greek world (Wheatley 2010). Nonetheless, this state of affairs was in a sense the high point of hoplite warfare, as it effectively made the Greek style of war the standard for armies across the entirety of the known world.

Although some local elements, such as war chariots or elephants, were used in their armies, and the amount of troops at their disposal dwarfed that of the old city-states, the wars of Hellenistic kingdoms (mostly fought with each other) generally stuck to proven Macedonian tactics. Indeed, Hellenistic armies largely abandoned Alexander and Philip's innovative tactics and, despite their varied troops, fell back on a heavy reliance on the phalanx and the sarissa. The confrontation between two orderly phalanxes was once again the deciding factor in most battles, in which the identical hoplite armies of the Hellenistic monarchs would be pitted against each during (Baker 2003: 379-381).

Phalanx warfare began to devolve into an impractical, overly-specialized arms race, with the sarissa growing even longer and more unwieldly, reaching up to 24 feet in length (Polybius, *Histories*, XVIII, 28-34). Although this did provide an advantage in a head-on charge against another phalanx, it also made the phalanx exceedingly difficult to maneuver, and incapable of fighting in all but the flattest of terrains.

At the same time, a new power was rising in the west. The Roman Republic, after defeating the former Phoenician colony of Carthage in the Punic Wars, came to fully control the Western Mediterranean, and began to expand its influence. The first Greeks to fall under Roman rule were the city-states of Southern Italy and Sicily. Rome then began expanding eastwards. The Romans began by interfering, like the Persians before them, in the internal affairs of the Greek city-states, before picking fights with the Hellenistic kingdoms themselves.

The Romans, however, had a new and devastating weapon at their disposal: the legion. In many ways, the legion was similar to the Greek phalanx, and there is little doubt that Roman military tactics and political organization owed something to Greek influence in Italy from the very earliest days of the Roman Republic (according to Roman tradition, the city was founded in 753 BCE). The Roman legion was a unit of heavy infantry, originally composed of trained, conscripted citizens, although it gradually grew more professional over time. However, as Polybius, the Greek historian who chronicled the rise of Rome and its triumph over the Hellenistic kingdoms, wrote, while the phalanx was invincible in a head-on charge, the Roman legion was far more flexible and manoeuvrable, and better suited for almost any type of confrontation that was not a frontal collision on a flat battlefield (Polybius, XVIII, 28-34).

It was the Roman legion that finally spelled the end of the dominance of the hoplite and the phalanx in the battlefields of Mediterranean civilizations. Key battles between Rome and the Hellenistic kingdoms and the leagues of city-states pitted Macedonian-style phalanxes against Roman legions. The battle of Cynoscephalae (literally "dog's head") in 197 BCE saw the first defeat of a Macedonian phalanx by a Roman legion (Polybius XVIII, 18-27) (Erskine 2010 "Cynoscephalae"). Also particularly important was the battle of Pydna, where the Hellenistic kings of Macedon were again defeated in 168 BCE. At that battle, the phalanx held its ground and seemed impenetrable by the Roman legions at first, but when the Romans fell back to more uneven terrain, the phalanx lost cohesion in pursuing them, and the Roman legions filled the openings left in the breaking ranks of the Macedonians. Ironically bested by Greece's mountains terrain, like the Persians had been centuries earlier, the Macedonian hoplites were defeated at close quarters as the Romans' heavy armament proved far more effective than the now comparatively light armor of the Macedonian hoplite and the impossibly long sarissa, which had almost become a ranged weapon (Livy, *Ab Urbe Condita,* XLIV, 40-42) (Erskine 2010 "Pydna). The battle of Pydna resulted in Macedon effectively losing control over the Greek city-states, and soon also losing its own independence (Livy XLIV, 43-XLV, 34).

Another key turning point was the sack of Corinth in 146 BCE, in which Rome defeated Corinth and its allies in the Achaean League, an alliance of Greek city-states (Livy, *Periochae* LII; Cassius Dio, XXI; Cicero, *Tusculanae Quaestiones,* III, 53) (Macky 2010).

The last of the Hellenistic Kingdoms to come under Roman control, however, was not in Greece at all. After the naval battle of Actium and the death of Cleopatra in 31 BCE, Ptolemaic Egypt, so called because of Ptolemy, the general who had inherited it after Alexander's death, became a Roman province (Cassius Dio, L) (Gurval 2010).

With these defeats, the last of the Hellenistic kingdoms came under Roman dominion, and the Roman Republic, soon to be the Roman Empire, was in full control of the Mediterranean, and effectively the known world. This spelled the end of political dominance for Greece, and also of the military dominance of their legendary hoplites.

## Online Resources

Other books about ancient history by Charles River Editors

Other books about ancient Greece by Charles River Editors

Other books about hoplites on Amazon

## Bibliography

Alcaeus, *Extant Fragments.* D.A. Campbell.1982. *Greek Lyric 1: Sappho and Alcaeus*. Cambridge, MA: Harvard University Press.

Archilochus, *Extant Fragments.* D. Gerber.1982. *Greek Lyric Poetry*. Cambridge, MA: Harvard University Press.

Aristotle, *Constitution of the Athenians*. H. Rackham. 1952. *Aristotle in 23 volumes (vol.23)*. Cambridge MA: Harvard University Press; London: William Heinneman Ltd.

Aristotle, *Politics*. H. Rackham, 1952. *Aristotle in 23 volumes (vol.21)*. Cambridge MA: Harvard University Press; London: William Heinneman Ltd.

Cornelius Nepos, *Life of Miltiades*. Watson, J.S. 1886. *Cornelius Nepos: Lives of the Eminent Commanders*. New York: Hinds and Noble.

Diodorus Siculus, *Library of History.* Oldfather, C. H. 1935. *Library of History*. Cambridge, MA: Harvard University Press.

Herodotus, *Histories.* A.D. Godley. 1920. *Herodotus, with an English translation by A. D. Godley*. Cambridge, MA: Harvard University Press.

Lysias, *Funeral Oration*. Lamb, W.R.M. 1930. *Lysias with an English translation by W.R.M. Lamb*. Cambridge, MA: Harvard University Press; London: William Heinemann Ltd.

Pausanias, *Description of Greece.* W.H.S. Jones, H.A. Ormerod. 1918. *Pausanias: Description of Greece*. London: Robert Hale Ltd.

Plato, *Menexenus*. Lamb, W.R.M. 1925. *Plato in Twelve Volumes, Vol. 9*. Cambridge, MA: Harvard University Press; London: William Heinemann Ltd.

Plutarch, *Moralia.* William W. Goodwin et. al.1874. *Plutarch. Plutarch's Morals. Translated from the Greek by several hands. Corrected and revised by William W. Goodwin, PH. D. Boston, Little, Brown, and Company.* Cambridge: John Wilson and son.

Plutarch, *Life of Alexander.* Perrin, B. 1919. *Plutarch's "Lives", 7*. Cambridge, MA: Harvard

University Press; London: William Heinemann Ltd.

Plutarch, *Life of Pelopidas.* Perrin, B. 1919. *Plutarch's "Lives", 5.* Cambridge, MA: Harvard University Press; London: William Heinemann Ltd.

Polybius, *Histories.* Shuckburgh, E.S. 1889. *The Histories of Polybius, 2 Vols.* London: Macmillan.

Thucydides, *History of the Peloponnesian War.* Jowett, B. 1881. *Thucydides translated into English; with introduction, marginal analysis, notes, and indices.* Oxford: Clarendon Press.

Tyrtaeus, *Extant fragments.* J.M. Edmonds. 1931. *Elegy and Iambus, with an English Translation by. J. M. Edmonds, vol. 1.* Cambridge, MA: Harvard University Press; London: William Heinemann Ltd.

Xenophon, *Anabasis.* Brownson, C.L. 1922. *Xenophon in Seven Volumes, 3.* Cambridge MA: Harvard University Press; London: William Heinemann, Ltd.

Xenophon, *Hellenica.* Brownson, C.L. 1922. *Xenophon in Seven Volumes, 1-2.* Cambridge MA: Harvard University Press; London: William Heinemann, Ltd.

Xenophon. *Cyropaedia.* Miller, W. 1914. *Xenophon in Seven Volumes, 5-6.* Cambridge, MA: Harvard University Press; London: William Heinemann, Ltd.

**Secondary Sources:**

Anderson, J.K. 1993. "Hoplite Weapons and Offensive Arms". In Hanson, V.D. *Hoplites: the Classical Battle Experience.* London, New York: Routledge.

Antonaccio, C. 2009. "The Western Mediterranean". In Raaflaub, K., Van Wees, H. *A companion to Archaic Greece.* Chichester, U.K., Malden, MA: Wiley-Blackwell.

Ashley, J.R. 2004. *The Macedonian Empire: The Era of Warfare Under Philip II and Alexander the Great, 359-323 B.C.* Jefferson, NC: McFarland.

Baker, P. 2003. "Warfare". In Erskine, A. *A Companion to the Hellenistic World.* London: Blackwell Ltd.

Brock, R. 2006. "Sparta, Athens and the Wider World". In Kinzl, K. *A Companion to the Classical Greek World.* Malden, MA: Blackwell Publishing Ltd.

Cartledge, P. 2010. "Messenia". In Gagarin, M., Fantham, E. *Oxford Encyclopedia of Ancient Greece and Rome.* London, New York: Oxford University Press.

Cartledge, P. 2013. "Hoplite/Politai: Refighting Ancient Battles". In Kagan, D., Viggiano G.F. *Men of Bronze: Hoplite Warfare in Ancient Greece*. Princeton: Princeton University Press.

Cawkwell, G. 1978. *Philip II of Macedon*. London, United Kingdom: Faber & Faber.

Cornell, T.J. 2002. "On War and Games in the Ancient World". In Wamsley, K.B., Barney, R. K., Martyn, S.G. *The Global Nexus Engaged: Past, Present, Future Interdisciplinary Olympic Studies. Sixth International Symposium on Olympic Research*. London, ON: University of Western Ontario, Canada.

Connolly, Peter. 2006. *Greece and Rome at War*. London: Greenhill Books.

Errington, R. M. 1990. *A History of Macedonia*. Berkeley, Los Angeles, Oxford: University of California Press.

Erskine, A. 2010. "Cynoscephalae, Battle Of". In Gagarin, M., Fantham, E. *Oxford Encyclopedia of Ancient Greece and Rome*. London, New York: Oxford University Press.

Erskine, A. 2010. "Pydna, Battle Of". In Gagarin, M., Fantham, E. *Oxford Encyclopedia of Ancient Greece and Rome*. London, New York: Oxford University Press.

Friend, J. 2010 "Military Structure and Organization (Greek)". In Gagarin, M., Fantham, E. *Oxford Encyclopedia of Ancient Greece and Rome*. London, New York: Oxford University Press.

Gruen, E.S. 2010. "Rome (Early Rome and the Republic)". In Gagarin, M., Fantham, E. *Oxford Encyclopedia of Ancient Greece and Rome*. London, New York: Oxford University Press.

Gurval, R. 2010. "Actium, Battle Of". In Gagarin, M., Fantham, E. *Oxford Encyclopedia of Ancient Greece and Rome*. London, New York: Oxford University Press.

Hale, J.R. 2013. "Not Patriots, Not Farmers, Not Amateurs: Greek Soldiers of Fortune and the Origins of Hoplite Warfare". In Kagan, D., Viggiano G.F. *Men of Bronze: Hoplite Warfare in Ancient Greece*. Princeton: Princeton University Press.

Hansen, M.H. 2006. *Polis: an Introduction to the Ancient Greek City-State*. Oxford: Oxford University Press.

Hanson, V.D. 2000. *The Western Way of War: Infantry Battle in Classical Greece*. Berkeley, Los Angeles, London: University of California Press.

Holland, T. 2006. *Persian Fire: The First World Empire and the Battle for the West*. London: Abacus.

Holt, F.L. 2010. "Alexander the Great". In Gagarin, M., Fantham, E. *Oxford Encyclopedia of Ancient Greece and Rome*. London, New York: Oxford University Press.

Heckel, W. 2006. In Kinzl, K., *A Companion to the Classical Greek World*. Malden, MA: Blackwell Publishing Ltd.

Krentz, P. 2013. "Hoplite Hell: How Hoplites Fought". In Kagan, D., Viggiano G.F. *Men of Bronze: Hoplite Warfare in Ancient Greece*. Princeton: Princeton University Press.

Lazenby, J.F. 1993. *The Defence of Greece 490–479 BCE*. Warminster: Aris & Phillips Ltd.

Lee, J.W.I. 2006. "Warfare in the Classical Age". In Kinzl, K. *A Companion to the Classical Greek World*. Malden, MA: Blackwell Publishing Ltd.

Macky, E. "Achaea and the Achaean Confederacy". In Gagarin, M., Fantham, E. *Oxford Encyclopedia of Ancient Greece and Rome*. London, New York: Oxford University Press.

Nafissi, M. 2009. "Sparta". In Raaflaub, K., Van Wees, H. *A companion to Archaic Greece*. Chichester, U.K., Malden, MA: Wiley-Blackwell.

Nimchuk C. 2010. "Persia (Achaemenid)". In Gagarin, M., Fantham, E. *Oxford Encyclopedia of Ancient Greece and Rome*. London, New York: Oxford University Press.

Potts, Albert A. 1982. *The World's Eye*. Lexington, KY: The University Press of Kentucky

Quinn, M.F. "Warfare (Greece)". 2010. In Gagarin, M., Fantham, E. *Oxford Encyclopedia of Ancient Greece and Rome*. London, New York: Oxford University Press.

Raaflaub, K. A. 2013. "Early Greek Infantry Fighting in a Mediterranean Context". In Kagan, D.; Viggiano G.F. *Men of Bronze: Hoplite Warfare in Ancient Greece*. Princeton: Princeton University Press.

Ray, F.E. 2011. *Land battles in 5th century BCE Greece: a history and analysis of 173 engagements*. Jefferson, NC: McFarland.

Roberts, J. 2007. *Oxford dictionary of the classical world*. London: Oxford University Press.

Sekunda, Nicholas. 1998. *The Spartan Army (Elite Series #60)*. Oxford: Osprey Publications

Singor, H. 2009. "War and International Relations". In Raaflaub, K., Van Wees, H. *A companion to Archaic Greece*. Chichester, U.K., Malden, MA: Wiley-Blackwell.

Tritle, L.A. 2010. "Peloponnesian Wars". In Gagarin, M., Fantham, E. *Oxford Encyclopedia of Ancient Greece and Rome*. London, New York: Oxford University Press.

Tsekhaladze G.R. 2009. "The Black Sea". In Raaflaub, K., Van Wees, H. *A companion to Archaic Greece*. Chichester, U.K., Malden, MA: Wiley-Blackwell.

Viggiano, G.F.; Van Wees, H. 2013. "The Arms, Armor and Iconography of Ancient GreekWarfare". In Kagan, D., Viggiano G.F., *Men of Bronze: Hoplite Warfare in Ancient Greece*. Princeton: Princeton University Press.

Vaughn, P. "The Identification and Retrieval of the Hoplite Battle-Dead". 1993. In Hanson, V.D. *Hoplites: the Classical Battle Experience*. London, New York: Routledge.

Wheatley, P. 2010. "Diadochi and Succesor Kingdoms". In Gagarin, M., Fantham, E. *Oxford Encyclopedia of Ancient Greece and Rome*. London, New York: Oxford University Press.

Wheeler, E.L. 1993. "The General as Hoplite". In Hanson, V.D. *Hoplites: the Classical Battle Experience*. London, New York: Routledge.

Williams J.M. 2010. "Lelantine War". In Gagarin, M., Fantham, E. *Oxford Encyclopedia of Ancient Greece and Rome*. London, New York: Oxford University Press.

## Free Books by Charles River Editors

We have brand new titles available for free most days of the week. To see which of our titles are currently free, click on this link.

## Discounted Books by Charles River Editors

We have titles at a discount price of just 99 cents everyday. To see which of our titles are currently 99 cents, click on this link.